I0625923

His Redemptive Story

Pastor Ronald Randle

Copyright

His Redemptive Story

Copyright 2025 Ronald Randle
ISBN: 978-1-958356-51-7

Forward

To them, God willed to make known what are the riches of the glory of this mystery among the Gentiles: which is CHRIST IN YOU, the hope of glory.

Colossians 1:27 (NKJV)

Within our lives lies the hope that God will redeem us. HIS Redemptive Story draws our attention to the testimony God has given us that He has redeemed us, and HIS STORY of such Redemption has given us the testimony accompanied by HIS BLOOD that enables us to overcome the enemy of our souls.

In this book, Pastor Ronald Randle challenges us to examine our lives and walk by faith rather than sight. I have lived and worked among many people who profess CHRIST, but I have rarely encountered someone with identical traits, such as a man of faith. Pastor Ronald Randle, however, has undoubtedly displayed a lifestyle of one who has been redeemed and found worthy to share HIS REDEMPTIVE STORY effectively.

Hand me the microphone, Pastor Randle, so I may cry loud and spare not because I am ready to shout about HIS REDEMPTIVE STORY!!!

Bishop Dr. Foley A. Parker

Forwards Cont'd

His Redemptive Story is a book of life, love and liberation. It's a personal honest and open look at the restorative power of God to change and reclaim the life of an individual for His purpose.

Pastor Randale shares his personal spiritual journey of struggles, failures and forgiveness that shaped his relationship to serve the Living God.

This book demonstrates the Sovereign Grace of God that delivers and empowers the weak and willing to be transformed into a vessel of honor for Divine Destiny. The prophet Jeremiah reminds us that God has investment in our lives, *"For I know the thoughts that I think toward you, saith the LORD, thoughts of peace, and not of evil, to give you an expected end. (Jeremiah 29:11 KJV)*

In so many ways, as you will read, Pastor Randale has lived a life of dealing with and overcoming adversity, and may his story inspire a new generation to fulfill their earthly assignment by God's Grace and Power.

Superintendent James Mason, MA
Imani Temple of Temecula, Pastor

Forwards Cont'd

Pastor Randle's book is a great read and I highly recommend it!

In it he lays out clearly the essence of what Jesus did for all of us on the cross!

He is honest in his expression of the ups and downs in his own life and the victory that can be found through the renewal of the mind through God's Word!

Once you start reading this book you will find it hard to lay it down and when you finish, you will be strongly encouraged by the inspirational truths in its pages!

Pastor Drew Koen, Senior Pastor
Hope Community Church
Pico Rivera, California

Forwards Cont'd

According to Pastor Ronald Randle, faith that is not tested can not be trusted. This is an amazing truth that sets a stage for a disciplined Christian living.

Every character in the bible from the old and new testaments were people whose faith in God were tried, tested and commended for their faith. They were men and women like you and me. They were weak, and not without faults but their faith and character changed the world. It made kings bow, and preach the gospel with all boldness.

Faith in God's word becomes a genuine and real faith when it is translated into a solid and dependable character that God and people can trust to build their lives on.

I believe God led Ronald Randle to write a true story of amazing and real faith and the experience of salvation and true freedom from sin, self-indulgence, dependency on self-knowledge and facing the risk of being destroyed by moral catastrophe.

The fact remains that people have written lots of books and stories of their experiences and achievements through sports, music, politics, leadership, marriage and family. Yet Pastor Randle's book about God's redemptive power through Christ is a remarkable story that the world needs to hear for liberation and radical transformation.

This book has such a powerful anointing. It truly describes the life of a man delivered from the deepest, filthy and dark pit of slavery, bondage and hopelessness. God heard his cry, saw his tears and miraculously brought him out, placed his feet on a solid and holy ground to stand and gave him a new song to sing.

His Redemptive Story is a testimony of the power of the cross and the cleansing blood of Jesus Christ confirmed with clarity and presents a true picture of Randle's forgiven past, present reality of a changed life, and the glorious hope of Christ's appearance.

I recommend that you read this book as a wonderful redemptive story that tells about the power of the gospel of Jesus Christ for all people regardless of nationality, cultural background, color of skin, denominations and social status.

Therefore, as you read this book, read it with confidence. It will help to guide you in taking complete charge of your destiny by faith in Christ. The fact remains that Jesus saves and forgives a vilest sinner. The greatest secret in all of life's endeavors and success is to hear God's voice calling you to accept Christ as God's gift for salvation and eternal life.

Thank you, Randle for hearing God's voice and yielding to His call of redemption. Thank you for giving us this life-changing testimony and principles as written in this book.

Pastor Evangelist Tage Swallie
World Mission Church
Liberia, Africa

Contents

Dedication

This book is dedicated to the pioneers of the faith in my personal life that enabled me to develop and grow in grace.

There have been men and women of God on the road who have invested in my personal life knowingly and unknowingly by myself.

The love of my covenant family, who demonstrate – to me – the love of God in my self-imposed nonsense and through that love, I've been able to see my purpose.

Destiny, Dorema and Daniel, who will one day, I hope, see the value of their love.

To the memory of the man of God who discipled me, Bishop George Dallas McKinney who never gave up, even when I didn't see. My Sister Jackie, through the Holy Spirit, prayed for me in my Lo-debar experience, which is a very desolate place.

Also, in memory of Roy Gunnar for his valuable contributions to the reestablishing of my faith.

Introduction

Love

On the subject of love, genuine love is an attribute of God that not everyone has experienced. Receiving the atonement of Christ through faith is the beginning of accessing the relationship of covenant love with the Lord. The actual nature of God is love.

Human nature loves with conditions, but the Divine nature of love is unconditional. II Peter 1:3 (KJV) *"According as his divine power hath given unto us all things that pertain unto life and godliness, through the knowledge of him that hath called us to glory and virtue."*

Love is what causes all who enter time to search for purpose and work toward eternity, to struggle together to make life meaningful, and to obtain a right relationship with God, the Father, through Jesus Christ.

God was in Christ reconciling us back to Himself. Now Christ is in us, desiring that we love humanity back to God.

I John 3:1 (NKJV) *"Behold, (which means to stop and truly pay attention), what manner of love the father has the bestowed upon us, that we should be called the sons of God:*

1

Therefore, the world doesn't know us because it didn't know Him."

This love the Father enables us to participate in, through His divine nature, baffles humanity and human's ability to comprehend. The same God who can cause a black cow to eat green grass and produce white milk has given us all things that pertain to life and godliness.

Be very careful because when one has been in church for a while, there is a tendency to forget what it was like on the other side. They fail to share God's love with someone in dire need of that love. John 15:12 (KJV) *"This is my commandment, That ye love one another, as I have loved you."*

Life is meaningless without purpose, and the yearning inside of me to have a meaningful life with purpose was put in my heart by the love of God. Abandoning myself to His gift of love enables me to rest or cease from trying to accomplish anything on my own, but through faith and His redemptive love, "I can do all things through Christ that strengthens me." Roman 5:5 (NIV) says, *"And hope does not put us to shame because God's love has been poured out into our hearts through the Holy Spirit, who has been given to us."* The King James version says, *"to be shed abroad"*, which literally means to be dumped out. It's the word used for the outpouring of the Spirit.

Christendom would have a whole different perspective if we could truly ascertain the depth of God's love for humanity. God gave us His best. He gave Himself in the person of Jesus Christ. God's love floods our innermost being when one truly rests in His redemption. What's amazing is God created all things for His purpose. For His glory, they are and were created. Revelation 4:11

So, we have access to sociable, intimate and personal relationships that enable us to experience the first institution ordained by God, which is marriage between a man and a woman, but His love supersedes the beauty of this intimacy. It does show us the necessity of carrying out these relationships in a moral and responsible way. God's love gives us the responsibility to respond the right way.

It is through repentance and brokenness that I've been able to forgive myself for abandoning the family God blessed me with. I was married on March 4, 1992, after being released from prison, serving four and a half years of an eight-year sentence, which could have landed me in prison for life, but the love and mercy of God enabled me to experience His grace.

After three children and eleven years of marriage, I abandoned my wife, who married me by faith, and my children, and struggled with unforgiveness and addiction, off and on, for Twenty-one years.

It has been because of the love of God in their hearts that I didn't reach the bottom of the pit. I can't begin to imagine what it has been like for them over the years, but they demonstrated forgiveness and love to me during the final stages of my struggle, watching me and loving me through it. I am grateful and humble today because of the God kind of love that was demonstrated and was instilled in them. They may never know what it did to and for me.

Today I am restored and made whole, walking by faith in the fruition of God's redemptive love. I realize that on this journey, as the scripture teaches in *Proverbs 24:16 (NKJV) "A just man falls seven times and rises again…"* Thank God that I can see times I've fallen and *I* was able to get up, but that was some of the problem. *I* got up.

Psalm 40:1-2 (NKJV) records, *"I waited patiently for the LORD and He inclined to me, and heard my cry. He also brought me up out of a horrible , out of the miry clay. And set my feet upon a rock, and established my steps."*

Love lifted me this time it was not on my own. I give God the glory for His mercy and His redemptive love.

Martin Luther King, Jr. said, "I refuse to accept the cynical notion that nation after nation must spiral down a militaristic stairway into the hell of thermonuclear destruction. I believe that unarmed truth and unconditional love will have the final word in reality. This is why right temporarily defeated is stronger than evil triumphant."

It looks like evil is advancing beyond love, and grace, but in the final round, righteousness will run down like water and justice will be like a mighty stream.

Daily affirmation: Good and right affirmations are more important and powerful than the evident evil.

Chapter One

The Process Precedes the Promise and the Promotion

The Process

It was during the process, which spanned more than two decades, when I learned that the message I preached at the beginning of my journey was to me. In many ways, the sermon I delivered on Elijah casting his mantle on Elisha, 1 Kings 19:19-21, was a prophetic synopsis of the life I would lead. I didn't understand that at the time because I was still developing into the man I am today. Even though I didn't know what was about to take place in my life, the enemy saw the light around me and the mantle I was being trained to carry and sought to destroy me.

   1 Kings 19:19-21 (KJV)

19 - So he departed thence, and found Elisha the son of Shaphat, who was plowing with twelve yoke of oxen before him, and he with the twelfth: and Elijah passed by him, and cast his mantle upon him.

20 And he left the oxen, and ran after Elijah, and said, Let me, I pray thee, kiss my father and my mother, and then I will follow thee. And he said unto him, Go back again: for what have I done to thee?

21 - And he returned back from him, and took a yoke of oxen, and slew them, and boiled their flesh with the instruments of the oxen, and gave unto the people, and they did eat. Then he arose, and went after Elijah, and ministered unto him.

Beginnings

I was the sixth of twelve children with eight brothers and three sisters. Even though my mom wasn't a constant churchgoer, she believed in God and the benefits of church as a hub of the community. I was baptized around four years old and went to church with my aunt who was a devout Christian. Although I didn't understand the significance of being baptized, I recognize now the importance of the command; being instructed as a little boy to be baptized.

When my aunt passed away, going to church and Sunday school was no longer a given on Sundays and soon became second to many things in life. Instead of a confidant, the Lord became more like an old friend that I moved away from and only spoke to on occasion.

My aunt wasn't the only person who actively tried to get us to focus our energy on positive endeavors. Around that time I came in contact with Archie Moore and became a member, as were many other youth in our neighborhood to join Archie Moore's ABC Club. I learned three different disciplines which

taught moral, spiritual, and physical self-defense. These disciplines today have profound value in who I am as a person, with a better understanding of the investment. I have carried two of the quotes he'd recite to us every day.

The ABC of Archie Moore (1971)

> ➤ All of the flowers of all the tomorrows are in the seeds of today.
> ➤ Even the humblest worker, when moved by the Holy Spirit, touches invisible chords that vibrate and make melodies throughout the eternal ages.
> ➤ When a task has begun, never leave it 'til it's done. If the task be great or small, do it well or not at all.

Growing up in the late 60s and early 70s, I became a very rebellious young man, searching for my identity and purpose. I was an easy vessel of manipulative men who searched for truth in lies. I was paralyzed by self-imposed nonsense a.k.a. sin.

Proverbs 23:23 (KJV) Records:" *Buy the truth, and sell it not; also wisdom, and instruction, and understanding.*"

To buy the truth is to invest or purchase, not travel by it but spend time or invest to receive the benefits of knowledge which is light and understanding. The only way to purchase truth is to invest in truth. You have to abide in truth to get what is accessible and available.

I spent time with men whose truths could be proven by conceptualizing certain parts of society. For instance, their

7

truth was that Caucasians were evil, shouldn't be trusted, and therefore should be hated. Then I was sent to certain parts of town for which *we* were hated due to stereotypes, prejudice and bigotry.

I remember at age eleven, knocking on the door, selling candy; a small child of around three or four came to the door and called out to his mother, "Mom, there is a nigger at the door."

This kind of statement and name-calling caused damage to my heart. As a young man, how do you filter that type of information? It didn't cause fear but rebellion towards society and those abusing their authority.

Instead of being taught discipline and character, I became hateful—vengeful—rebellious toward society as a whole. The demonic influences came from the systemic racism that had been employed through deception. At age thirteen I began experimenting with drugs and rebelling against authorities. Drugs quickly became a way of life.

Chapter Two

Self-Control

Self-control is one fruit of the Spirit that we can attain through yielding to the Holy Spirit. I believe it's important also to examine what causes a lack of this attribute.

2 Timothy 2:16 (KJV) *"But shun profane and vain babbling: for they increase into more ungodliness."* So, as we are listening to things that are not edifying and building us up. We are allowing things that don't edify and build up to get into our spirit.

We are in an age of information. Some of it righteous and some of it evil. There is a difference between righteousness and wickedness. Knowledge in Him will guide you into all truths. John 16:13

This is where the Christian thinks they know the power of deception when the bible says this increases ungodliness.

1 Corinthians 15:33 (KJV) *"Be not deceived: evil communication corrupts good manners."*

Proverbs 25:28 *(NKJV) "Whoever has no rule over his own spirit, is like a city broken down, without walls."*

Can a person control evil? No. This is why we must avoid foolish and vain babbling.

9

The root cause of all of our problems is that we reject God's way.

"All we like sheep have gone astray; we have turned every one to his own way; and the Lord hath laid on him the iniquity of us all." Isaiah 53:6 9KJV)

The root can bring forth fruit that's not pleasing to God and makes its opposition to God all the more obvious when conviction arises. Defensiveness exposes and magnifies what has taken root inside. It can surface in the form of the following: anger, rage, fury, indignation, emotional excitement induced by intense displeasure, emotional reaction, loss of self-control, and the boiling over of feelings.

Anger can breed resentment, threatening looks, or speech which is the outward manifestation, which causes a reaction and also loss of self-control.

Looks, acts or words that often suggest a greater exhibition of feelings, temper or mood.

Because of examination and observation of what has taken place through my own experience, it shows an area that's very important for us to exercise authority over. After a short period, one can demonstrate repentance and receive restoration, it is easy to recuperate physically but spiritually the battle begins to intensify; the flesh and the spirit war against one another.

(Being mean-spirited or planning retaliation is not an option when we suffer an injustice or are hurt or offended.) (John Bevere)

Scriptures to study for self-control

1. Psalm 119:165 (KJV) *"Great peace have they that love thy law and no thing shall offend them."*
2. Proverbs 30:33 (NIV) *"For as churning cream produces butter and as twisting the nose produces blood, so stirring up anger produces strife."* Anger and strife caused the floodgates of sin to overwhelm us.
3. Proverbs 12:16 (NIV) *"Fools show their annoyance at once but the prudent overlook an insult."* Wisdom causes us to look beyond the fault and see the need.
4. Proverbs 14:29 (NIV) *"Whoever is patient has great understanding but one who is quick-tempered displays folly."* Patience allows us to think and use wisdom, but being quick-tempered causes shame.
5. Proverbs 19:11 (NIV) *A person's wisdom yields patience; it is to one's glory to overlook an offense."*

Being patient demonstrates wisdom, especially over trivial things. This shows long-suffering and self-control. Failing to demonstrate self-control reminds me very much of past situations that could have been avoided if a sensitivity to yield had been exercised.

The emotions and feelings of disrespect don't produce faith; the kind of faith that overcomes adversity and anger. The fruit of Spirit is love, joy, peace, kindness, meekness, temperance, faithfulness, and self-control; against such, there is no law. (Gal 5:22-23)

We must be ever mindful of Christ's love which enables us to have authority and power over the wiles of the adversary. "The weapons of our warfare are not carnal but mighty through God to the pulling down strongholds that try to exalt themselves against the direction in which one is headed which is in deeper love with Christ." (II Corinthians 10:4-5)

Forgiveness is the genius of the Christ-like faith. It's what God did through Christ on Calvary to bring redemption so that we may be restored to the right relationship with Him.

So not holding one hostage, one can experience forgiveness and grow in grace and God.

1 Corinthians 13: 1-2 (NKJV) *"Though I speak with the tongues of men and of angels but have not love, I am as a sounding brass or a clanging cymbal. And though I have the gift of prophecy and understand, all mysteries and all knowledge and though I have all faith that can remove mountains, but have not love, I am nothing."*

God is love and this is the divine attribute in His nature. He enables us to experience and share. We desire to love as God loves. I know that I haven't arrived but I have also been living in this earth suit long enough to understand something about myself.

In the process, I became broken and realized that my gifts took me where my character didn't keep me. I'm grateful for God's grace and mercy and His word which teaches me that the gifts and calling of God are irrevocable which tells me, man might change his mind, but God is sure and does not change his mind. (Romans 11:29)

Philippians (KJV)1:6 *"Being confident of this very thing, that he which hath begun a good work in you will perform it until the day of Jesus Christ:"*

So, continue to grow in grace and love – agape love.

In the process of working on embracing the mystery of His love, which is His divine nature, He allows us to participate with Him in the work. God wants more than anything for us to experience the ultimate intimacy with Him. We often sing the song, "I Want to Know You." It's very difficult to know anyone without a relationship. Acknowledging now, more than ever before, this is what God desires of us.

John 14:23 (KJV) *"...If a man love me, he will keep my words: and my Father will love him, and we will come unto Him, and make our abode with him."*

Chapter Three

(S.I.N.) Self-Imposed Nonsense

Proverbs 25:28 (NIV) *"Like a city whose walls are broken through is a person who lacks self-control."* When you have no self-control, it causes restraints to be gone. To be conflicted causes sin's doors to be open.

When I was fifteen, I was arrested for armed robbery while still in the store. I was sentenced to twenty months in the California Youth Authority (CYA). Occasionally churches would come to minister, but I wasn't falling for any of that. It had been instilled in me that Caucasians were hate-filled and their picture of Jesus had blond hair and blue eyes, something I could not identify with.

Ron Randle, the sneakiest base-runner around

San Diego Highschool
Annual, 1975

A little over a year and a half later when I came back from the California Youth Authority, I was bigger and more educated but my mind was still firmly planted in rebellion.

I was good at sports, so when I got out of CYA I was recruited by several universities for baseball and

14

football. I was encouraged but going away to school would mean leaving familiar surroundings.

I decided instead to go to a junior college where I excelled on the football field until my rebellious attitude caused a lack of discipline and I was injured on the practice field on the last day we were in pads. Now I was not only looking at a promising future sift through my fingers, I was in pain from both

San Diego Union Tribune, October 17, 1974

the physical and emotional injury. An injury I would eventually nurse with pain pills that led me back to a path with drugs and fueled my hatred even more.

So, I turned my back on society, my education, football and a future that seemed as mangled as my injured knee and committed myself to a life of drugs and crime.

The rebellion placed me on a destructive path with a group of others and we ventured into the world of drugs and crime.

When I was released eleven months later, I returned to the life of drugs and crime but this time the consequences of my actions were more than I could handle.

The adversary will take you further than you want to go and leave you there longer than you want to be there.

I was unknowingly exposed to Angel Dust and my mind went out to lunch for five years. This is not to say that I didn't

15

know what I was doing or that I have no recollection of that time. Still, I was not fully in control of my emotions or will. I was erratic, mentally unbalanced and caught up in a cycle of destruction that would take decades to get out of.

Some made the statement, "He's crazy."

I'll tell you, I was past crazy.

But God had a purpose for me.

Today, understanding the dynamics of warfare, the devil's plot was to destroy me but God's purpose was to shield me.

My very being was chemically altered. I spent time in more than one county mental health facility. I would hear voices and be overwhelmed by bouts of fear. I longed for the time when I had full control of my mind.

I graduated from high school in 1975 with a 3.7 average, but I wouldn't walk with my class to receive my diploma.

One day I put my graduation gown on and walked from 38th and National to 25th and Imperial, stopping at every church along the way. I walked into a church on 32nd Street which happened to be in the middle of their service and strolled right up into the pulpit and sat down, telling them that I wanted to give my testimony. *I had no clue what a testimony was at the time.*

After I disrupted them one too many times and some words were exchanged, I was ushered out and I continued my walk. I ended up in a Muslim Temple on 25th and Imperial Ave. where I sat and talked to the Imam.

In 2007, the year I planted the church, Faithwalk Covenant Church of God in Christ, I was led to go back to the church where I'd interrupted service during my long 'walk'. I walked in and asked if I could speak to the pastor. As I was sharing the story with him and a few other men, a young man of 38 years of age stood up and asked me if I had been wearing a blue robe. It turns out that he was in attendance that day thirty years before. I then had the honor of listening to him give his first sermon and participating with him in his call to the ministry.

All of history had to line up for me to come face-to-face with that young gentleman as I was at that moment. It served as a tangible, 30-year witness to the fact that what the enemy meant for evil regarding my life, God turned to good.

Mind you, the church planted on 37th and Oceanview Blvd. in 2007, was on the very street where I was stabbed. In an attempt to escape, my assailant, fell from a two-story building, landing on the concrete in 1983. Pastor Marvin Davis's daughters lived downstairs. Upon finding me, they called an ambulance. The next thing I remembered was waking up in the hospital.

The next Sunday I was at the altar of his church.

As I think about it now, I would say that I gave the enemy an opening to destroy me, but his failure is definitely God's glory. If the enemy knew how much I would use the things I learned during that time in my warfare today, he would have worked harder to remove me from this earth.

Two women came into my life at that time. I knew one from an early age, both Christians. They prayed for me and took me to church. They showed me love. There was no judgment or condemnation. They looked beyond my faults to who I could be in Christ even while the PCP-induced voices remained, and I kept doing drugs. It no longer mattered what the drug was; if it was in front of me, I took it. Still and yet, the mothers prayed for me.

It was as if this brief brush with being introduced to Christ had alerted Satan. *This one is not going to get away*, Satan probably vowed.

A person who is numbing pain will not use drugs for the sole purpose of pleasure or leisure, but those with addictive personalities become paralyzed. Satan knows where you've been because he took you there. He doesn't know where you are going because he is not God, but he will try to keep you stagnant and keep you from going forth in Christ.

When a person has an encounter with God there's salvation that takes place. There is a process of development and growth. Oftentimes, the body, which should be part of the development, is lulled to sleep. There is a nurturing and developing aspect of being born again and the church (body) is to help develop the person's spirit, emotions and body.

The adversary's objective is to hinder that development because once that person is delivered, they will bring others with them.

For years I did the adversary's bidding but God's mark was on me and His light surrounded those who prayed for me. This was enough to keep the enemy's attention on me.

Chapter Four

Faith

Faith (pistis) in the Greek [I trust Him] which means firm persuasion, a conviction based upon hearing (to persuade) always of faith in God or Christ or spiritual things.

Romans 3:25 (NIV) *"God presented Christ as a sacrifice of atonement through the shedding of His blood to be received by faith…"*

Faith in redemption through Christ produces God-like character and love that demonstrates our salvation. Since we have been justified through faith (just-if-ied) we can again be restored to a right relationship with God. Hebrews 11:6 (NKJV) *"Without faith it's impossible to please Him for we who come to God must believe that He is and that He is a rewarder of them who <u>diligently</u> seek Him."*

Forsaking all, I trust Him, not depending on anything or anyone except Christ who I can believe and trust. Not to say that we do not have fellowship with those who have this like-precious-faith but that we are being led by the faith of Christ.

Hebrews 4:14-15 (NIV) *Therefore since we have a Great High Priest who ascended into heaven. Jesus the Son of God let us hold firmly to the faith we profess, for we do not have a*

High Priest who is unable to empathize with our weaknesses, but we have one who has been tempted in every way just as we are yet He did not sin." (No self-imposed nonsense.) This means He's touched by our afflictions, our pain, our sickness [sorrows] but these don't move God. He is moved by our faith.

Hebrews 11:1-3 (NKJV) *"Now faith is the substance of things hoped for, the evidence of things not seen. ² For by it the elders obtained a good testimony. ³ By faith we understand that the ʲworlds were framed by the word of God, so that the things which are seen were not made of things which are visible."*

How can we examine faith without being mindful of the Father of faith? Abram was willing to step out on nothing in obedience obeying God without asking who, where, when, or how leaving at the call of God and wandering in the wilderness to a land promised but not seen or envisioned. He was also willing, by faith, to sacrifice his promised seed Issac symbolic of Christ which by faith enables us to receive the promise. Now known to us as Abraham. Now faith is the actual intangible substance when exercised with the leading of the Spirit. It's amazing how little trust most Christians actually have in the true omnipotence of God and the gift He allows us to participate in.

James 1:17 (KJV) *"Every good gift and every perfect gift is from above, and comes down from the Father of lights, with whom there is no variation or shadow of turning."*

No principality, power, spirit or entity. God has given us the ability to create as well as speak things into existence as He did.

Mark 11:22-24 (NKJV) *"Have faith in God. For verily I say unto you, that whosoever shall say unto this mountain, be thou removed, and be thou cast into the sea; and shall not doubt in his heart, but shall believe that those things which he saith shall come to pass; he shall have whatsoever he saith. Therefore I say unto you, what things soever you desire when you pray believe that you receive them and you shall have them."*

Notice that Jesus says, whosoever shall say, not whosoever doesn't say, but the one who says (according to the will of God). Whatsoever you desire when you pray, believe that you receive them and you shall have them. Faith is believing the not yet, right now. *Now* faith is...

So, if there is a mountain in your way…and I don't mean Mount Rushmore or Mount Cuyamaca but Mount Doubt, Mount Fear, Mount Addiction, Mount Sickness, Mount Low Bank Account or whatever the mountain; speak to your mountain and it will move from your life.

But when you stand, praying for forgiveness; if you have aught, anger, bitterness or resentment against anyone, your Father in heaven won't forgive your trespasses. If you do not forgive neither will your Father forgive your trespasses. (Mark 11:25-26)

This is why it's so important to rest in His redemptive love with a repentant heart. When one has faith, one can step out on nothing and still embrace everything. There is nothing that is made or exists without Him. God's kind of faith and love causes you to have a repentant heart and be transformed. This enables the hardened heart to open the door. Notice that the doorknob is on the inside.

Revelation 3:20 (KJV) *"Behold, I stand at the door, and knock: if any man hear my voice, and open the door, I will come in to him, and will sup with him, and he with me."*

Hebrews 10:22-23 (NIV) *"Let us draw near to God with a sincere heart and with full assurance that faith brings. Having our hearts sprinkled to cleanse us from a guilty conscience and having our bodies washed with pure water. Let us hold unswervingly to hope we profess for He who promised is faithful."*

Without the anointing of the word washing our minds with divine truth, we will not be able to truly rest in redemption. Faith involves the acceptance of God's love and when God's love is in us then it must find an outward expression.

James 2:17 N(KJV) *"Thus also faith by itself, if it does not have works, is dead."*

Ephesians 2:8 (NKJV) *"For by grace you have been saved through faith, and that not of yourselves; it is the gift of God,"*

Faith that is not tried and tested is faith that cannot be trusted. Both naturally and spiritually.

The first test was failed. The day God told Adam and Eve that they could eat from every tree but the tree of knowledge of good and evil for it could so easily beset them. He told them if they did, they would (die which would) be spiritually separated from Him.

Chapter Five

God's Great Grace

January third of 1988 was the first Sunday of that year. I came to church and at the time of the altar call stepped before the minister at the altar.

He asked me, "What are you here for?"

The only thing that came out of my mouth was the word deliverance. I didn't know what deliverance was at the time. It was just what came out of my mouth. It was what God wanted for me and what I wanted for myself even though I didn't know how to express it. He did.

Later I found out that the "Devotion for that Day" in the "Your Daily Bread" article on January 3, 1988, was, "Deliverance for those who are bound in sin." This spoke volumes to me in the process.

This is how this gift of deliverance was presented to me.

For the next four days after my church visit, I was sober and hopeful that *I* had finally gained control. Then I came in contact with a friend who had also spent time in the world and the church.

Within two weeks we were arrested. This time for seventeen counts of robbery, two of which were kidnap-robberies. The two kidnapping counts each carried a twenty-five-year prison term.

I was now in a place where God could keep my attention.

Two devotionals became daily reading, *The Days of Praise* and *Daily Bread*.

It was then that I saw my arrest as an act of God's grace. A grace that continued. Instead of getting fifty years, I received eight, of which I served four and a half. Still, it wouldn't matter how much time I spent incarcerated, it was the time I invested with God in that facility. And instead of going to *do* time, God sent me there to *invest* my time—in Jesus. Ultimately, my circumstances didn't change, my heart did. In my heart was the seal of the Holy Spirit.

God shaped and molded my mind and heart in preparation for one of the greatest gifts I have received from Him – my covenant wife, Theresa.

A friend of mine on the outside suggested I begin writing to a young lady, Theresa. With her encouragement, I wrote to her and after several months without a response one afternoon I received a letter, and to my surprise it was her. My response was to go to the phone and call her. And in my communication, I asked her to marry me.

I had never seen her. I had no clue what she looked like. I believed God and because of the trying of my faith and my development, God knew where my heart was.

When I still had eighteen months to go, she came to visit me. The caption under the picture I had taken was "Love perfected in Christ Jesus."

The very day that I got out of prison, March 4, 1992, we were married and Faithwalk became a reality. March 8, 1992, I submitted to the work of the Lord at St. Stephen's Church of God in Christ and my life changed for the better.

As long as I was diligently walking and praying in the spirit and walking in obedience all was well.

There is a danger of being lulled to sleep if you are not purposefully and intensely studying, reading and praying. Moving in carnality while being able to do the job, you lose sight of the warfare and you begin trying to do spiritual battle in the flesh, which is not truly possible.

From 1992 to 1996, with a burden for drug addicts, prisoners, and hurting souls, I held Bible studies in prison facilities, at honor camps, and at the San Diego Rescue Mission.

I soon recognized that I was under the leadership of one of the greatest men I have ever met and probably will ever meet, Bishop George Dallas McKinney. He was a family man, a scholar, a teacher and a preacher but foremost he was an anointed man of God who revered God, whose heartbeat for the souls of God and strived to live holy.

He was also one of the few men of God I've known to build character and faith in men of God through demonstrating godly character and faith.

He endeavored to raise up mighty men of God so they could go out from under his leadership, become shepherds as well, and raise up more mighty men of God.

I recognize today that Bishop McKinney demonstrated to me what it was like to live a Christ-like life. That was who he was and it took a while but I finally realized that it was what I desired and who I am today.

God gave me a leader to follow who once again, demonstrated to me the character of true leadership, servanthood with a vision of God. Only our paths to knowledge, understanding and surrender were vastly different.

What I recognize today is that **you can't give something to someone that you don't have, and you can't teach something to someone that you don't already know**.

Bishop McKinney, being a learned man, knew the scripture, knew God, knew how to lead men to God, and even how to counsel men who had given over their control to drugs, alcohol and other pleasures of the flesh (self-imposed nonsense). He helped me and others surrender their lives to Christ, but Bishop McKinney didn't know first-hand what it was like to have his mind go on vacation for four to five years because the introduction to angel dust was an invitation to hell. He didn't know how any controlled substance, no matter its intended initial benefits, shackled waiting to be placed back on one's wrists.

None of this is an excuse. It is simply a fact and the path of life I was led to live to show those who don't think God can't rescue, receive, redeem, or recover them where they are.

My wandering was not God's perfect will but in discipline and development, the Spirit of God began to remind me that we grow in grace. Titus 2:11-12 *"For the grace of God that brings salvation has appeared to all men, teaching us that, denying ungodliness and worldly lusts, we should live soberly, righteously, and godly in the present age."* **Grace exclusively belongs to God.** *Man has no heaven nor hell to put anyone in.*

The Grace of God is for all men and God in His Grace, suspended the rule of judgment for me. There were many times when my body and mind wanted to give up. I even asked God to stop the rotation of the world and let me off. But He extended His grace and said, "No."

Being delivered is not the same as being made whole. The only way we become whole is in Christ. This way we operate in the dominion that was given to us where the dominion has rule over all (self-imposed-nonsense).

My next prison was more sophisticated than any physical prison. You are locked up in your mind. The warden is fear.

Chapter Six

Humility

I suppose I have warred against the subject of humility because of the rules and regulations of men who are persistent in humiliating others to cause their egotistical efforts to bring the discipline desired by God. Such humiliation can cause injury, offense and indignant behavior.

The humility I do understand is Godly and brings true repentance and Christ-like love which yields growth and character.

Based on Colossians 2:20-23 (NIV), *"Since you died with Christ to the elemental spiritual forces of this world, why as though you still belong to the world, do you submit to its rules. Do not handle, do not taste, do not touch. These rules which have to do with things that are all destined to perish with use, are based on merely human commands and teachings. Such regulations indeed have an appearance of wisdom with their self-imposed worship, their false humility and their harsh treatment of the body. But they lack any value in restraining sensual indulgence."*

Godly humility comes from agape love because God was faithful, and a man of God, Joseph, did not want to expose

Mary to public disgrace after he considered it, then the angel of the Lord appeared to Him in a dream. (Matthew 1:20)

There is a noise that one must overcome when there is pain produced by purpose. The only way Joseph could hear was by resting in the redemptive purpose for all humanity.

Being humble is a virtue that consists in the absence of pride. God resists the proud but gives grace to the humble. Humbleness of mind, humility – tapeinophrosune, primarily signifies how being in low posture is always used in the right sense. The absence of pride in oneself or achievements is a consciousness of one's weakness and disposition compared to God. Our supreme being. Undoing self - depreciation or humiliation, Christ enables us to rest in His redemptive love and shows us the example through His obedience by dying on the cross. *"Nevertheless, not my will but Yours, be done."* (Luke 22:42 NKJV)

Never less than God's best, Matthew 11:28-29 (NIV) *"Come to me all you who are weary and burdened and I will give you rest take my yoke upon you and learn of me, for I am gentle and humble in heart and you will find rest for your souls."* I am not saying rules and regulations are not good in the training of discipline but self-imposed matters supersede the God-given purpose. Ego eases God out then it causes offense, injury and indignant behavior, understanding that every soul is subject to the governing authorities.

Human intellect does not give the right to overlook the Spirit of Truth. 1 John 2:27 states that the anointing that you have received will teach you concerning all things and you need not that any can teach you. This doesn't mean that we are not to adhere to instruction guidance, constructive criticism from leaders in the faith, fathers in the faith, brothers and co-laborers, but if we want to know something, the anointing of the Spirit of Truth can and will teach us. It's amazing how understanding can be misunderstood by a person who is misunderstood. In other words, a person can have a conviction that's wrong and believe it's right or true when all the time it is selfish and deceptive to understand is to stand under God's law.

Psalm 19:7 (KJV) *"The law of the Lord is perfect, converting the soul; The testimony of the Lord is sure, making wise the simple."*

The Word is our manuscript, living and powerful. It's the word that became flesh, humbling Himself, becoming obedient to the death of the cross so that we could be redeemed from the sentence of eternal damnation. It's plain what's stated by scripture.

Romans 14:22 (NIV) *"So whatever you believe about things keep between yourself and God. Blessed is the one who does not condemn himself in what he approves."*

The latter of verse 23 states, everything that does not come from faith is sin. So, this means if something is offensive to a brother or sister one should not expose them if they are offended by it or it causes them to stumble. Let's not examine to humiliate, to degrade, demean, embarrass, or to discomfort. Often, it's not what is said but how it's said that takes a whole different meaning.

31

Philippians 2:3-5 (KJV) "*3Let nothing be done through selfish ambition or conceit, but in lowliness of mind let each esteem others better than himself. 4 Let each of you look out not only for his own interests, but also for the interests of others. 5 Let this mind be in you which was also in Christ Jesus,*"

God's thoughts are higher than our thoughts and His ways are also higher as well (Isaiah 55:8-9), but He does allow us to participate with Him in repairing souls and the ministry of reconciliation.

Buildings are torn down and rebuilt often, but the house of this tabernacle is an ongoing construction and damaged seed produces damaged fruit. This is why it's so important for men of God to be Christ-like.

II Corinthians 3:4-6(NKJV) "*And we have such trust through Christ toward God.5 Not that we are sufficient of ourselves to think of anything as being from ourselves, but our sufficiency is from God, 6 who also made us sufficient as ministers of the new covenant, not of the letter but of the [a]Spirit; for the letter kills, but the Spirit gives life.*"

Every seed produces after its own kind so we must be circumspect in our sowing because evil produces after its own kind. So many people are hurt in church because of folk who are in a position of authority who don't rightly divide the word of God.

You can read all day long but if you don't put application to what you know, you will not progress well.

Information and education do not bring true salvation. Without revelation you don't have salvation, you just have accumulated facts.

Do not compromise for a bigger vote or check. You are sacrificing lives and one day it will be your own.

How does one share with someone in his own ego when true repentance and humility are brought by God? God will offer wisdom with pure love where men take their own ego and stroke themselves and not the person who needs to be restored.

Wisdom with pure love allows the brokenness of feelings and emotions that were caused by abuse of power, language, and authority, to heal.

Jesus said in John 6:63 (KJV), *"...The flesh profiteth nothing. The words that I speak unto you, they are Spirit and they are life."*

In conclusion, it's the desire of my heart to walk in full fruition of why He called me to the ministry.

Ministry is the God-given ability to give to others what God has given to you. I'm so glad God still hears a sinner's prayer. I had given up, ready to catch the stagecoach without a crown. I could be dead in my grace but I'm grateful that God demonstrated His redemptive love so that I could still be here to rewrite the end of the story for my good, but for His glory.

When the word is allowed to be the word (smothering the noise of man), there is healing and life.

Even the humblest of workers when moved by the Holy Spirit touches invisible chords that vibrate and make melodies throughout the eternal ages. ~ Learned from Archi Moore as a student.

Never again in life will I allow my personal pride or people to paralyze my purpose.

Chapter Seven

Discipline and Growth

As an armor bearer or adjutant to a leader with such a demand on his anointing as Bishop George Dallas McKinney, I found myself amongst the higher echelon of the Church. Church, meaning, leaders of not one or two denominations but many organizations coming together to advance the Kingdom of God.

Bishop McKinney was an ecumenical leader. The robes were stripped and shirt sleeves rolled up in pursuit of spreading the Gospel in the most effective way possible.

Soon after, Bishop McKinney was elected to the General Board of the Church of God In Christ, Inc., to serve as one of twelve members governing a Pentecostal organization. As his armor bearer, I traveled with him, sat in meetings as an invisible sponge, and attended conventions and meetings I otherwise would not have been able to participate in.

I also witnessed things in the spiritual and natural I was not mature enough to handle then, but today would have dealt with this spiritual warfare differently.

Just because it looks like someone higher up in the hierarchy or with more years following God can get away with sin, doesn't mean it is so, and it definitely doesn't mean that you can. And I could not.

If you are casual in your walk with Christ, it will cause casualties in the Body of Christ.

My Bishop, a man who sought God's heart, strived to live holy and preached Holiness, was surrounded by men who I thought should have been less carnal. My first misstep was in examining them, the second was judging them and my third was engaging in my own sin, not understanding that God could see it in the midst of the deception around me.

My time under the leadership of Bishop McKinney, though it spanned more than 30,000 hours, was abbreviated by being lulled asleep and then surrendering to drugs. The recurring pain from a knee injury decades before drew me to painkillers which slowly set me back on the road to controlled substances and any other fleshly desire. I turned to a relationship outside of my marriage- I ended up with all of Egypt coming back into my life when I had already been delivered.

Being let go from his employ in 2003, was like being on a high dive that I jumped off of into a cesspool of sin.

I was bound again in my own self-imposed nonsense. It was a spiritual prison for 21 years off and on.

40th Psalm (NKJV), *"I waited patiently on the Lord; and he heard my cry. He also brought me up and also out of a horrible pit, out of the miry clay."*

Some people talk about pulling themselves out but the only one that can pull you out and keep you out is the Lord.

Being called without being fully prepared to wait on your calling causes you to fall into a cycle of chasing a plan instead of waiting on God for your purpose. It takes a process of maturing that is also needed to prepare you for the ministry God has for you.

I stepped out thinking I was ready just because some of my ministry was revealed but I wasn't ready for the attack.

When you aren't ready for a spiritual attack you are susceptible to anything.

I didn't realize that in sitting under Bishop McKinney and being shrouded by his mantle, his enemies became my enemies. The evil forces being fought in spirit warfare couldn't be conquered with the flesh. I was on the front line as his armor bearer which meant I had to stay in the spirit. But I tried fighting with my carnal nature and human intellect.

The best thing I can say about my character at that time was, that I never prayed or laid hands on anyone at the pulpit or during altar call when I wasn't in right standing with God.

Later that year, I made a phone call to one of the saints. In the midst of my brokenness and addiction, she took me to Bishop McKinney's house. That evening I was enrolled in Teen Challenge, an organization that rebuilds broken lives.

I must say that I am thankful. God faithfully takes us where we have to go, then He meets us there and brings us forth—from darkness to sunlight—to meet and minister to others so that we might help others by giving them what He has given to us.

He also sets forth a way for redemption and uses those who listen to bring us back to Him.

Wisdom delivered with pure love allows healing to be received wholly.

Chapter Eight

Forgiveness

Forgiveness, the genius of the redemptive Faith. Forgiveness is a subject that needs to be examined by every born-again believer. I believe forgiveness is the genius of our faith. First looking at the word forgive the Greek word of this means to send away to remit or forgive debt. Being completely canceled. The deliverance of the sinner from the penalty of death. This remission is based on the proprietary sacrifice of Christ, atoning, sacrifice and forgiveness.

The God of creation stepped out of eternity into time, imparted the spirit of himself into the womb of a virgin and became flesh. Here enters Christ. John 1:1 (KJV) *"In the beginning was the word, the eternal logos, and the word was with God and the word was God.* John 1:14 (KJV) *And the word became flesh and dwell among us, and we beheld his glory. The glory of the only begotten son of the Father, full of grace and truth."* The word became flesh so that flesh could be conformed back to the word. Once it's conformed to the word, it can be transformed by the word.

Without the shedding of blood, scripture teaches there is no remission of sin. The bloodshed on Calvary was pure because man had no participation in the conception. God allows man to participate with Him in most construction of life. But He won't let man mess Grace up. Grace exclusively belongs to God. Every man and every woman that is born is conceived in sin because of the sin of the first man. We are all born on death row. This was why God's atonement through Christ is so deep. Because of His willingness to forgive all of humanity, Christ's redemptive power of love, His blood removes the offense and puts us back in the place with God before the offense. Right standing with God. The righteousness of God in Christ.

God's love, (Romans 5:8) was demonstrated in this; "that while we were yet sinners, Christ died for us." We are all God's children through creation, but only we who are born again have the right to be called sons and daughters. We are children not born of natural descent, nor human decision or the husband's will, but born of God. John 1:13 (KJV) *"who were born, not of blood, nor of the will of the flesh, nor of the will of man, but of God."*

Love and forgiveness were demonstrated to me through the mother of my children and my son and two daughters after abandoning them, and being unable to forgive myself because of decisions, and addiction I struggled with for over 21 years. Their willingness to receive me in their home and love me through the mess for the first time truly enlightened me to this revelation of God's redemptive Covenant of love. It showed me how his atonement was so powerful that we could be at one with him in an intimate relationship.

This atonement requires repentance. 1 John 1:9 (NIV) *"If we confess our sins, God is faithful, and just to forgive us of our sin and to cleanse us from all unrighteousness."* This is what enables us to come boldly to the throne of grace and obtain mercy and find grace to help in time of need.

My question was why do I need to find Grace when I'm already saved by Grace through Faith?

God's redemption at Christ's expense.

That it's the simplicity of the gospel that saves but simple salvation does not cover every situation. We need grace for healing and we need grace for forgiveness. Grace for deliverance. We need grace for specific situations. Another word in the Greek 'charisma' means to bestow (fix) a favor unconditionally – used as an act of forgiveness through repentance and confession, there is no limitation to Christ's law of forgiveness.

David was considered to be a man after God's own heart. (I Samuel 13:14, Acts 13:22). David, I believe shared an intimacy with God that gave him rare favor, but as a man, he caused brokenness in his relationship with God. But from this exposure of his nakedness and sin by the prophet Nathan, and David's repentance, he penned the 51st. Psalm verse 1. *"Have mercy upon me O Lord, according to your loving kindness, according to the multitude of thy tender mercies."*

His mercies are new every morning. We are not dependent upon yesterday's mercies, but brand-new mercies every morning. Blot out my transgressions, wash me thoroughly from my iniquity and cleanse me from my sin. Vs. 6, *"Behold, thou desires truth in the inward parts, but in the hidden part, thou shall make me to know, wisdom."* Teach me truth in such a way that my past will not again impact my future.

The sin which originally took place and happened in 2 Samuel 11:1 The Bible stated that this was a time when Kings went out to war but David stayed home. If David had gone to Battle, he would not have seen Sheba on the rooftop. From this seed of disobedience came adultery, murder, death of a child, rape, and also the loss of a son, but through his repentance was born Solomon, the wisest king.

There are many modern examples of men of God being exposed. The word is clear. In Proverbs 28:13 (NKJV) is recorded, *"He who covers his sins will not prosper, But whoever confesses and forsakes them will have mercy."*

The word Teshuvah means to repent or return to a state of moral purity and goodness. The scholars ascertain this meaning by connecting the word to a change of heart or disposition. A change of mind or purpose, man, emphasis for man on the change of conduct. Mostly God's repentance because of rebellion and disobedience.

Genesis 6:6 (KJV) *And it repented the Lord that he made man on the Earth, and it grieved Him at His heart."*

Genesis 6:8, (KJV) *"but Noah found Grace in the eyes of the Lord.* There are times when God desires to build character and romance a genuine love relationship with man that will cause him to repent of the discipline he pronounces. He will also expose evil and sin should one continue. The Lord doesn't change His mind toward evil. But our God is merciful.

Forgiveness to repentance and Godly sorrow.

When we begin to deal with the eternal Spirit of God, we begin to deal with everything because everything came from God.

Christ said from the cross, "Father, forgive them for they know not what they do" (Luke 23:24). In the act of forgiveness, we are free from others, renting space in our heads and hearts with no intentions of paying rent. Jesus had our well-being in mind when he made it a requirement for us to walk in forgiveness. Unforgiveness works more destruction against us than on the one who may have offended us.

To lay aside the sin (self-imposed nonsense), the weight, the pain, the anger and bitterness, to avoid spiritual quicksand, forgiveness is the key element in any type of healing, whether physical, emotional or spiritual. The power of forgiveness enables us to rest in His divine redemptive love.

Chapter Nine

Challenge and Redemption

I remember leaders making empty promises that would hold me hostage to my past. They did this to humble me. These same leaders tried to deal with me with a long-handled spoon.

After not being able to acquire an assignment in California through the Teen Challenge Ministry Institute, I spoke to a man of God who was a part of the Church of God in Christ. Our spirits connected and he suggested I talk to the director of (Pacific Northwest) P. N. W. Teen Challenge.

In obedience, I spoke to the gentleman. He let me know that he was hiring for a couple of positions but he would pray about it and would consider it.

He didn't get back to me right away due to the scheduling. I remember being discouraged due to the judgment of men I thought were my peers. It caused me to sequester myself with God, growing closer to Him, listening to Him, being uplifted by Him and waiting on Him.

I had worked in the church for over eight years before going through Teen Challenge. I thought this made me more than qualified to carry out the assignment I believed I had been given, but I needed to wait for God's clearance. The highest form of clearance there is.

We are called to wait but the posture in which we wait can make all the difference. One can wait with an attitude of gratitude.

God allowed me to endure the contradiction and hostility to rid me of my fear of man and look only to Him for my promotion.

When I went to Washington in July 2019, I arrived a few days before beginning the assignment as education coordinator.

There was a young man who started his journey to recovery under my tenure. We both grew together at that starting point. Today the young man is a staff member at the facility where he was reconciled to a right relationship with God. Also giving to others what the Lord has given to him.

My assignment as the education coordinator was to teach the curriculum of Teen Challenge. I was to provide the curriculum and structure each phase so that the men could complete the process of recovery and growing in grace. So, it was more than a job, it was an assignment.

My ministry is to set men who are bound by their own self-imposed nonsense (SIN) free. These men aren't all necessarily locked up behind bars. They are locked up in their hearts and minds. They are locked up in their house (the temple (the body) where God desires to dwell through the Spirit of the resurrected Son).

We have people who have set up doorbell cameras at the front of their homes because they won't come to the door due to fear. They have given control to the emotions they have derived from what they watch and see on television. They are both desensitized by what they have been bombarded with and fearful that they too will be abused. This is the elevation of the fear factor when what is needed is prayer – Spiritual Warfare.

Time with God is the only way to heal their wombs, calm their minds, bring them peace, and make them whole. We as a people are to be restored to God which was Christ's intended purpose. Not to be imprisoned, by sentencing, fear, drugs or desires of the flesh. We are to be redeemed back to the Father,  made whole, and operate in the dominion that was given to us. Often, many experience deliverance but are not made whole.

For me, 1992 to 1996 was a training ground in the process, while participating in bible studies in prison facilities, at honor camps and the San Diego Rescue Mission. In 2003 I again succumbed to the control of substance abuse and was bound again by my own self-imposed nonsense (SIN).

Having been on both sides of this classroom allowed me to be aware of how to communicate with these men. With an idea of the inner workings of the curriculum, and what I had been tasked to do, I instructed these men in the Word of God.

46

I would have scriptures around the room that weren't in the curriculum. I didn't add to the curriculum; I merely taught them scripture.

Just imagine. I have a group of young men. They don't know how to forgive, and they are in pain. They need peace. Psalm 119:165 (KJV) says, *"Great peace have they which love thy law: and nothing shall offend them."*

You have a group of young men who don't know where they're going or why they exist. They don't have an inkling of how to get out of their situation. So, you lead them to the only One who could take them out of darkness, if they invested time with Him.

Bishop McKinney, being the man of God that he was, humble enough to share with the very students that I was assigned to after being a student under his leadership, visited the group via Zoom one morning.

One of the young men who sat in on that meeting with Bishop McKinney is now the teacher of that class and another is the director of that program. Even though they didn't recognize the quality of the leader Bishop McKinney was, they remembered him.

The director let me know that under my tenure, there were more graduates from this facility than at any other time. That encouraged me.

In September 2020, I contracted COVID and was bedridden for so long that my sick leave and paid time off ran out. I returned to San Diego and the wife *I* chose to marry, trying to recreate what the Lord had done so many years before – on my own – created a more intense level of warfare. This was not God's perfect will for me, but I was allowed to enter His permissive will and it cost me dearly.

I should have realized when we first separated that I was being allowed to take another path, but I stood by *my* word and we reconciled, getting a place together at the beginning of 2021.

Once again, I slipped back into addiction, due to the social demands surrounding the beginning of my relationship and the truth of the matter. I brought us together. Not God. So, I didn't have the emotional support I needed to move smoothly through the transition from one year to the next. At the end of the year, there is a lot of transitioning. Going into the new year can be hard for some people.

At the beginning of 2023, I was off the wagon and into full-blown addiction again.

When you stop chasing drugs, drugs chase you.

This time though the people surrounding me wouldn't let me forget whose I was.

Before I moved in with my wife, I stayed with a mother of the church, helping her with errands and driving her around. I would also take her to see her son who was in a coma.

Even in my addiction, I would see about her. One day, while I was driving her around, she put a CD in the car to play. It was a recording of me preaching. I sat there listening as I preached to myself.

Shortly after I heard that tape, I went to Teen Challenge. Yet, that didn't stop me from falling again.

When I got tired of the path I was on, I looked for another path. I was so tired. I asked the Lord, "Stop the World and Let me off." I had come to the end of that journey.

I was done.

I was tired of the pain and unforgiveness. I was tired of disappointing myself, my children and all of those who had invested in my life. I was tired of the bitterness, the anger, the resentment and the abandonment. I was just done.

In February of 2023, when I went to reestablish the discipline of my faith, I went to a different facility. I didn't go through Teen Challenge. They wanted me to start all over. Instead of being in a place of spiritual discipline, it would have been a spiritual prison for me.

Their curriculum treats everyone the same, but I needed someone to go to war for me and with me. I didn't need a program, I needed discipline and spiritual warfare. I was fighting for my soul.

This school is simply disciplined learning from the teacher. The teacher doesn't show up until the students appear.

February 13, 2023. I checked into a detox facility for five days. I came out then and went into the program. I was there to reestablish the discipline of my life away from drugs and everything else that had me bound. I was there for 50 days.

The Board Burdened Burning Ceremony went on for three days. Every psychological, emotional, mental, pain, abuse and

addiction that tied me to the past was burned and severed. I can't speak for anyone else, but from that moment I've never been the same.

Even today, I have a relationship with the director.

Romans 14:23 "…Anything that is not of faith is sin." But as we begin to study, you have to remember that there is natural and spiritual warfare.

2 Timothy 2:15 (KJV) *"Study to shew thyself approved unto God, a workman that needeth not to be ashamed, rightly dividing the word of truth."*

Chapter Ten

Power

When first asked to write on this subject, what came to mind was the Hebrew word for power: Dunamis (dynamite) power is the ability or might sometimes metonymy of persons and things. But first and foremost there is God whom this passage refers to, Ephesians 1:21 (KJV) reads, *"Far above all principality, and power, and might, and dominion, and every name that is named, not only in this world, but also in that which is to come."*

When we look at this verse regarding the name of Jesus, there has been a lot of controversy and complex conversations as to which translation is correct and which way we should identify Him. Before we understood what letters and vowels to place in which order there was the whisper of His, God's, spirit to ours. Our spirits recognized Him first and communed with Him long before He gave us a verbal and written identifier. This is why He is above every name we could utter. There is more power in His spirit communing with ours than us giving Him a token of acknowledgment by voicing the identifier without purpose.

1 Corinthians 1:18 (KJV) *"For the preaching of the cross is to them that perish foolishness, but unto us which are saved it is the power of God."*

Romans 1:16 (KJV) *"For I am not ashamed of the gospel of Christ: for it is the power of God unto salvation to every one that believeth; to the Jew first, and also to the Greek."*

In order for us who are being transformed to truly understand power we must reexamine redemption, the redeeming power of God through Jesus Christ enables us to participate in the divine exchange. Christ is once and for all taking our unrighteousness and exchanging it for His righteousness.

Hebrews 9:12 (NIV) *"He did not enter by means of the blood of goats and calves, but He entered the most holy place once and for all by His own blood thus obtaining eternal redemption."* The power of the redemptive act was wrought by love which is the main source of power, not a resource but how can we make Him known without knowing Him?

But the actual foundation from which the deliverance and freedom arrived. God's redemptive love is so powerful, I understand now we've only been scratching the surface of how deep. He desires true intimacy with us. His power of love supersedes any human capacity to relate without the Spirit of Truth and the ability He gives us to abide in His divine covenant of His love.

Hebrews 9:13-14 (KJV) *"For if the blood of bulls and of goats, and the ashes of a heifer sprinkling the unclean, sanctifieth to the purifying of the flesh:[14] How much more shall the blood of Christ, who through the eternal Spirit offered himself without spot to God, purge your conscience from dead works to serve the living God?"*

The Greek word (exousia) denotes freedom of action; when the right to act and be used by God in absolutely unrestricted authority. Authority is delegated by God.

Colossians 2:8-10 (NKJV) *Be not deceived by philosophy or empty deceit according to the tradition after the rudiments of this world and not after Christ. For in Him dwells the fullness of the Godhead bodily, and we are complete in Him who is head of all principalities and powers."*

In Christ's love, we have been given the authority and ability or power to exercise this same spiritual gift of divine power to rest in Him. This is where preeminence presides over the beggarly elements and the darkness that tries to exalt itself above the word of God. The Word is quickened and made alive in us so it can operate through us.

In our brokenness, we experience the power of love in The Way. The subject of power in scripture may be viewed under the following heads. Its original source is the Godhead. God the Father in creation, God the Son in redemption, and God the Holy Spirit in preservation. Its government is the Kingdom specializing in manifestations of divine power, past, present and future.

Power exists in created beings. Other than man there is no other inanimate nature. This was committed to man and because of the fall and deception, it is misused by him.

Also, power that's committed to believers through the Spirit of God, is indwelt by Him and will bring glory to God. II Peter 1:3-4 (KJV) *"³According as his divine power hath given unto us all things that pertain unto life and godliness, through the knowledge of him that hath called us to glory and virtue:*

⁴Whereby are given unto us exceeding great and precious promises: that by these ye might be partakers of the divine nature, having escaped the corruption that is in the world through lust."

This mystery which was hidden ages past has now been made known to those who seek Him wholeheartedly and participate in this divine intimacy and fellowship, God is love and He desires a love relationship based on the fulfilled desire of Him, not on keeping rules. The mystery of love involves a mutual reciprocation of two hearts that cherish each other and want to live in harmony together. Out of that love, they are willing to accept any conditions placed on the relationship to avoid disrupting the harmony they enjoy.

Redemption brings us back to this kind of love and relationship with God. The word mystery in Greek is musterion, which actually means secret information communicated to those who are initiated.

This can be made known only by divine revelation and is known in a manner at a time appointed by God. And to those only who are humbled by His Spirit.

Colossians 2:2-3 *"²That their hearts might be comforted, being knit together in love, and unto all riches of the full assurance of understanding, to the acknowledgment of the mystery of God, and of the Father, and of Christ; ³ In whom are hid all the treasures of wisdom and knowledge."*

My heart goal is that we may be encouraged and united in love so that they may have the fullness of complete understanding so that we may know the mystery of God, namely Christ in whom are hidden all the treasures of wisdom and knowledge.

The mystery of divine love and the godliness he has enabled us to participate in defies human intellect. To abide in this grace and redemption means to remain or stay in. The communion is so powerful it causes us to abide in brokenness when we through the power of the Holy Spirit understand the power of love that made this possible.

Proverbs 1:7 (NKJV) *"The fear of the Lord is the beginning of knowledge but fools despise wisdom and instruction."*

Carnal or worldly fear is false evidence appearing real.

II Timothy 1:7 (NKJV) says *"God has not given us a spirit of fear but of power and of love and a sound mind."* Only through the power of the grace of God can we be forgiven and released from the power of sin that caused us to be born on death row.

Job 14:7-9 *"For there is hope for a tree if it can be cut down. That it will sprout again, and the tender branch thereof will not cease."*

We are trees of righteousness (the planted of the Lord). If we (the tree) do not produce fruit, we become dormant.

"⁸ Though the root thereof wax old in the earth, and the stock thereof die in the ground;"

Yet, the Word of God (water) can revive the root and cause the tree to bud and bear fruit again.

"⁹ Yet through the scent of water it will bud, and bring forth boughs like a plant."

John 14:6 (KJV) *"...I am the way and the truth and the life and no man comes to the Father but by me. As the Way,* He is the path to the Father. As the *truth* He is the reality of all God's promises, and as the *life,* it's because of Him that we live and move and have our being.

When one sees He is the way, we've entered into time. When we see He is the truth, it's His story, and when we see He is the life, everyone will spend eternity somewhere. Death to eternal damnation and life to Eternal life.

Like myself, put down the pen and trust the Author, who is the Author and the finisher of our faith. (Hebrews 12:2).

Chapter Eleven

Rebuilding, Restoration and Replenishing

When I came back to San Diego, I continued to practice the discipline that helped me free myself from some of the control I had given to drugs. Praying, staying in the Word of God and warring in the spirit set me back on the path God had set for me.

The vision that God gave me in 2007 started speaking to me very clearly. I started instructing young men. Reestablishing the discipline caused me to see where I had come from. I was adamant about not being called a Christian but being Christ-like. Christians killed their wounded. Being Christ-like takes discipline. The great commission was to go into all the world and make disciples -- not Christians.

I do understand the communication concerning Christ-like behavior. The Body of Christ is an organism, not an organization. In organized religion, which is ritual and routine behavior, schools of learning have lost the diligent,

disciplined, and circumspect approach to rightly dividing the Word of Truth.

2 Timothy 2:15 The man or woman of God has been charged to study, not just stare and read; To be circumspect is to be careful. The spiritual war is moment by moment, not once a week.

The following is something that I have been employing in my walk and I continue to do for myself and others.

I instruct people on the path where they may have an encounter with God so that He can redeem them and rebuild their broken lives.

Through the authority of the Holy Spirit, who is the teacher, I am continuously willing to humble myself and submit to continual discipline and development of growth.

My life was broken but by applying the knowledge, or light of Christ, I'd acquired from His Word to my life and being a doer of God's Word, I have the confidence and boldness to minister, counsel and assist others in seeking an intimate relationship with God.

That is one of the dynamics of how God operates through us as believers and just not to know about Christ.

So I wait, write, watch and witness.

2 Habakkuk 1 (KJV) *"I will stand on my watch, and set me upon the tower and will watch to see what He will say unto me and I shall answer when I am reproved."*

For one to be reproved he had to first be approved, which means one is proven first. There is a process that comes with wholeness.

Verse 2 *"And the LORD answered me, and said, Write the vision, and make it plain upon tables, that he may run that readeth it."*

Verse 3 *"For the vision is yet for an appointed time, but at the end it shall speak, and not lie: though it tarry, wait for it; because it will surely come, it will not tarry.*

Acts 17:26 (KJV) *"And hath made of one blood all nations of men for to dwell on all the face of the earth, and hath determined the times before appointed, and the bounds of their habitation;"*

Today, as I look back over the process, the psychological and mental pain and much of the systemic racism I've encountered enables me to understand that there is one race; the human race. It is because of the Men of God and women of God of every culture who loved me through my self-imposed nonsense (SIN) that I am better today and able to provide the love of Christ.

Acts 17:30 (KJV) *"And the times of this ignorance God winked at; but now commandeth all men everywhere to repent:"*

True repentance produces the brokenness to obtain the promise.

My heart's desire today is to continue to grow in grace, rebuild broken lives and teach others to love like Christ loved.

John 17:11 (KJV) *"And now I am no more in the world, but these are in the world, and I come to thee. Holy Father, keep through thine own name those whom thou hast given me, that they may be one, as we are."*

Acknowledgments

To the saints of God whose prayers I stand on today.

The mothers who demonstrated a genuine mother's love but with spiritual labor pains: Mother Lily Trousdale, Mother Jean C. McKinney, Godmother Barbara Gunnar and Mother Eliza Sheppard.

To those whose encouragement could not be outmatched: Sister Alicia Roberson, Sister Pearl Barnes, Bishop J.A. Blake, Pastor Glenn McKinney, Elder William Days and Dr. Gwynn Taylor. Pastor Richard Dresselhaus and Pastor Drew Cohen.

Ned Banning and R. C. Eldridge, businessmen whose demonstration of Christ-like love and investment of time and resources has brought much encouragement.

Brother Ferman Whiteside for his love and encouragement.

Tye Waller, who shares with me the dichotomy of two life stories, one of discipline and one of rebellion. His discipline lifted him up the ranks of professional sports whereas my own rebellion landed me in the penitentiary.

In memory of Mother Mattie McAfee whose last words to me come back to me daily. **"It matters what you do with the gift."**

1 Timothy 4:17 (NKJV) "Neglect not the gift that is in thee, which was given thee by prophecy, with the laying on of the hands of the eldership."

Mother Barbara Gunnar's son, who was driving that day and witnessed the change in me, asked if I would mentor him. It just so happened that his father was one of my mentors in Archie Moore's ABC Club. I had the original brochure, and I was sharing with him about the Covenant, which is not a contract but an eternal agreement with God. (Psalm 25:14)

We looked in the sky and saw a rainbow over Mexico from where we were on 61st Street in San Diego. When we looked north the sun was shining. It was the first time I'd witnessed a rainbow in the sky and the sun shining where it hadn't rained in weeks. Mother Gunnar looked at me and said, "Son, you better follow your rainbow."

And still the confirmation, even until 2024 when I chose a card at the end of a prayer shut-in from the altar and it said, "Be a rainbow in someone's clouds."

This gift brought things full circle. In 1988 I was facing 50 years in prison, and in 2024 I received the gift of a 1988 Cadillac to begin working for the Lord.

About the Author

Pastor Ronald Randle was born in the city of San Diego in 1957. He is a graduate of San Diego High School. During his teen years, Elder Randle recalls being a vessel manipulated by men who search for truth in lies. In 1988, while facing a 50-year-to-life sentence in prison, he accepted Christ and was miraculously transformed by the power of the gospel. Pastor Randle ended up serving only four and a half years of a negotiated eight-year sentence.

In 1995 he was ordained and licensed as an Elder in the Church of God in Christ, and shortly began serving as Chief Adjutant to the Honorable Bishop George D. McKinney. Elder Randle was blessed to travel throughout the country with Bishop McKinney to the Holy Land, where he participated in bringing the word and sharing his testimony of deliverance. Pastor Randle has been involved in prison ministry and counseling to those in transition for over 31 years, part of which involved working with the San Diego Rescue Mission. The past struggles he has overcome have given him a strong foundation to bring deliverance to those who have been manipulated and lied to by the adversary.

In 1998 he was ordained by the Caribbean Christian Ministry, an international organization.

Today, Pastor Randle is an advocate for youth in the juvenile system where he was a product of both the California State Youth Authority and Prison. He operates in the office of a pastor, building a community of true worshipers.

If you'd like to get in touch with Pastor Randle, please call: 1(619) 648-9479.